TURNING POINTS
EMBRACING LIFE'S DEFINING MOMENTS

DINO RIZZO

ISBN 978-0-9764460-9-5
Published by Healing Place Productions, Baton Rouge, Louisiana

For further contact, email info@healingplacechurch.org
or write: Healing Place Church, 19202 Highland Road,
Baton Rouge, Louisiana 70809

Printed in the United States of America

I dedicate this book to my life's turning points:

First, to Jesus Christ, my Savior (June 21, 1982)
And to DeLynn, my beautiful bride (December 16, 1988)
To my incredible daughter, McCall (May 21, 1994)
And to my awesome son, Dylan (March 7, 1996)
And to my precious Isabella (November 7, 2000)
And to the amazing team and family
at Healing Place Church (December 1992)

ACKNOWLEDGEMENTS

F irst of all, I want to say thanks to the Healing Place Church staff and family. We have been on an exciting journey together for the last thirteen years, from our small beginning when John Osteen gave us our first offering. There were twelve of us in service the first week and after my sermon, only seven remained. But now, because of God's blessing, Healing Place Church is a multi-site church full of thousands of people who remain committed to the original passion to be a healing place for a hurting world. I thank God for giving DeLynn and me such a wonderful staff and church family to do life with.

Thanks to the staff who helped put this resource together. To Lance and Kari LeBlanc, David Song, and the rest of the Creative Group at HPC for the cover design and the interior art concept and layout. To Crystal Tullos for her input with the monologue in chapter five. To Johnny Green and Mike Haman for reading over and speaking life into this project. Mostly to Dan and Vicki Ohlerking without whose time and energy this would not have happened (thanks, "Rollerkings"). Also to the team that works side-by-side with me daily: Marc, Richie, Angie, Mark, Amy, Kristin, Jeffrey, Betty, Harmony, Juanette, Claudia and so many others that do what they do for an audience of one—Jesus.

Thanks also to all the friends that have been turning points for us—the team at BMC, David Meyer, Jr., Joyce and Dave Meyer, Nick and Christine Caine, and Carrol Gulledge (who gave me the Good News).

Thanks to my parents, Robert and Gloria Rizzo and DeLynn's parents, Wayne and Dee Austin. And finally to DeLynn, who is my lasting love. What a teammate she has been in our adventure at HPC. Her love for our children and me has been the staying power of this ride.

Thank You, Jesus, for all these gifts, but especially for giving Your life to me. You are my turning point.

CONTENTS

FOREWORD

I'm sure you've noticed that life is not perfect and predictable—not even for Christians. We all experience a variety of happenings in our lives—some happy, some sad, some exhilarating, some traumatic. I have certainly had my share of both good and bad experiences in life, and I can now see how each one played a part in the ultimate fulfillment of God's plan for my life and ministry. Along the way, I learned the importance of trusting God, who makes "all things work together for good to them who are the called according to His purpose" (Romans 8:28).

Trusting is not always easy when we are in the middle of very trying—sometimes desperate—situations, but even these times can be pivotal points that can make our lives better and improve our relationships with God.

In *Turning Points*, Dino Rizzo gives enlightening and uplifting messages of encouragement that will convince you that even difficult situations can be positive, life-changing experiences in your journey with God.

Dino is a man who continues to live the message of this book. That is what makes the pages of this book so powerful. If you apply these principles to your own life, you will not only get through the tough times, but you'll find new levels of intimacy with God.

The very things you thought would destroy you are the things God will use to catapult you into your destiny. If you need a significant change—a milestone moment—in your life, I encourage you to read these pages with an open mind and willing spirit. Let God make something incredible happen in your life.

Christine Caine
Hillsong Church
Equip and Empower Ministries
Sydney, Australia

PREFACE

J ust a few days ago I sat in my office looking out the window at a sky full of signs of more threatening weather on its way. Another dangerous hurricane was looming in the Gulf of Mexico, just hours away from hitting southern Louisiana. I started thinking how our state was in the middle of an amazing turning point.

We took an incredible beating from two hurricanes, Katrina and Rita, in a matter of just a few weeks. I witnessed some of the most tragic devastation I could imagine during the days following those two deadly hurricanes. I have seen serious devastation while on missions trips to India and Africa, but I never thought America would see such loss of life, human dignity, homes, jobs, hope, and peace. Tremendous pain and suffering landed right at our doorstep.

At the same time, I have seen God making His people stronger and more resilient than ever before. We'll never be the same again. The response of the body of Christ was

DINO RIZZO

13

phenomenal. Many times, government officials, community leaders, and even our own military told us that without the efforts of the churches in this region, much of what was done to save lives and property simply would not have happened. The church served as first responders in many situations, was dispersed to reach and rescue in the hardest-hit areas, and ministered to families and individuals affected by the storms.

My heart has been broken over and over again as I've listened to families tell how they managed to escape the rushing floodwaters and endured the frightening and frustrating ordeal of getting to a safe place, only to find out later that all their treasured belongings had been swept away in just a few hours. But even though there was so much sorrow, despair and exhaustion, there were still huge sparks of faith. Many people turned to God for help, and by His grace, He allowed us to be a part of His response to their need.

This experience has been a clear reminder to me that each person's story matters to God, and it should matter to us. Whether it is a father with his family in a shelter in southern Louisiana, a mother in India, or a senior adult in the Philippines, loss and pain is still loss and pain whenever and wherever it happens.

I find great strength in the truth of Romans 8:18 which says, *"I consider that the sufferings of this present time are not worthy to be compared with the glory which shall be revealed in us."* God cares greatly about our suffering, and He knows that there's something greater in store for us on the other side of our suffering.

Here's an entry from my blog three weeks after Hurricane Katrina hit:

> *Monday, September 19, 2005, 12:02am*
>
> *I've seen some great things come out of the tragedy of Hurricane Katrina. Not to minimize the pain and suffering at all, but I've seen the people of Healing Place rally hundreds of volunteers and hundreds of thousands of pounds of clothing, non-perishables, water, and everything else you can imagine. I've seen hundreds of local churches partner together with PRC Compassion to send thousands of volunteers and millions of pounds of goods into the relief area. Through medical equipment, generators, chainsaws, thousands and thousands of meals, hours of meetings, dozens of chaplains and trauma counselors, cots, bedding, prayers, smiles, and hugs, the body of Christ has been in the forefront from day one. No single church could have done this—it was just The Church. To God be the glory.*

The body of Christ has not been hiding during these trying days. Instead, we have emerged as an army of God, sent to deliver healing to hurting people. Early in this ordeal, we recognized that this was not just a natural disaster, but also very clearly a spiritual war. John 10:10 tells us that the thief—Satan—wants to steal, kill, and destroy. The destruction he seeks is souls. He wants to ruin souls, not just houses and homes.

Many houses and properties have been ruined because of broken levees. There has also been a breach in the spiritual "levees" people have built against any thoughts of their need for a Savior. That breach has created an opportunity for the church to step up and say, "This is why we're here—to provide healing and hope in Jesus' name."

I guess it really shouldn't amaze me—but it does—that the week just before Katrina hit, we called our staff at Healing Place Church to prayer each morning and to a day of fasting. Our prayer was that God would send us a harvest and that we would be prepared to take it in, whatever the cost. Little did we know how directly and quickly that harvest would be upon us. God knew that an important turning point for the church in southern Louisiana was imminent.

For the most part, the harvest didn't come knocking on the door of our church. Rather, we were presented with the chance to add feet and hands to our prayers by finding ways to help the victims of the hurricanes. Ministry at that point meant helping evacuate those who were in danger by cutting fallen trees out of their yards and roadways. Ministry was feeding them and giving them shelter and bottled water.

Praying with those needy, desperate people in the "black room" of the triage center at the New Orleans Airport, we found the harvest. In the midst of this terrible tragedy, there were so many hurting people, most of them helpless and hopeless. We did all we could to serve and show them the love that God has for them.

Another interesting aspect of those days is the fact that

we were about halfway through a series in our weekend services at Healing Place Church called, "Turning Points." We were looking at some of the moments in the life of Jesus and in our own lives that had been points of significant change. We also were learning how we could help others who are facing turning points in their lives. A turning point can be painful, but I have found that where there is pain, Jesus is always near. He likes to be with those who are hurting.

It may not be a hurricane or a disaster that compels you to embrace the turning point God has for you. It may be some other, more personal tragedy you've experienced. It may be a challenge you're facing as a parent. It may come in the form of an opportunity to help someone who is hurting. Or it could just be a chance for a fresh outlook on a new day.

I pray that the thoughts on the following pages will become a sanctuary that will fill you with hope and faith on your journey through your own personal turning point today.

To serve Him,

Dino Rizzo

INTRODUCTION

WHAT IS A TURNING POINT?

TURNING POINT:
The point at which a very significant change occurs; a decisive moment; a trigger; the beginning of a chain reaction or domino effect; a shift; a pivot.

TURNING POINT: *The point at which a very significant change occurs; a decisive moment; a trigger; the beginning of a chain reaction or domino effect; a shift; a pivot.*

Remember the timelines your teacher put up on the wall in World History class? The big dots on the timeline are history's turning points. They identify milestones in the development of our societies and civilization. Consider the scattering of mankind in the story of the Tower of Babel. In essence, when God shut down the construction site at Babel the world went from one language to what has grown to hundreds of thousands of languages and dialects today. Think about the births of Isaac and Ishmael. The world's most intense religious rivalry and the resulting wars with both sides fighting in the name of God were all there when Abraham fathered his two sons.

The worldwide spread of the gospel began with the missionary travels of the apostle Paul. The explorations of Christopher Columbus unveiled a whole new world, and Charles Lindbergh's flight across the ocean created tremendous opportunities in travel. In all of this, we can see how our entire world has been changed by the repercussions of relatively few events.

Technology has a history driven by significant turning points. Johann Gutenberg's press revolutionized the availability of information, as did the invention of movable type. A kite flying in a storm welcomed us to the world of electric power. And Thomas Edison's light bulb—how much did that one single invention change the world? Think about the changes to our cultures and lifestyles that came with each step in the development of communications. We went from the telegraph to the telephone, to radio, to television, to cell phones—and now to the mind-blowing worldwide connectivity of the Internet.

I know God didn't allow man to invent all this just so we could live more comfortably, but I am certainly grateful for the invention of indoor plumbing and air-conditioning (especially here in southern Louisiana). I love my iPod. I love TiVo. I love eBay. I love getting to live in a global community that has come about because of turning points in communication technology.

There are many different kinds of turning points. There have been economic turning points like the Great Depression. Political turning points often swing on tiny hinges, as we saw in the presidential election of 2000 when it all came down to a few votes in one Florida county. Wars often have battles that serve as turning points, like the invasion of Normandy on D-Day by the allied troops in World War II. Historians agree that this terrible, bloody day turned the tide of the European arena of the war.

Competitive sports at all levels are full of turning points. Basketball is one of the most momentum-driven games in the world today. One of the greatest abilities a basketball coach can have is to know how to control the momentum of the game. An appropriately placed time out can fend off a loss of momentum, and a well timed three-pointer or defensive stop can turn the game around. The psychological impact on the fans as well as the players is huge. And when fans start making noise, it can really make a difference in a game.

Let me give you an example. I grew up in the Carolinas, so I have always been a fan of the ACC (Atlantic Coast Conference). One of my favorite teams is the Duke University Blue Devils. I loved watching the "Crazies" in Cameron (that's what the hard-core Duke fans call themselves). Their seats at basketball games are close to the floor, and they stand up for the whole game doing synchronized cheers, taunts, and antics.

Recently I went to a Duke home game with my son Dylan, my father-in-law, and my brother-in-law. It was a great game. Duke was behind in the closing minutes and started making a comeback. The fans went wild every time the opposing team touched the ball, and it was obvious that the noise was bothering the opposing players. The noise the crowd was generating in their excitement caused a turning point in that game. Duke won, largely attributable to the outrageously noisy crowd. I loved every second of it. Dylan and I became "Cameron Crazies." We were part of the making of a turning point in the momentum of a basketball game.

Movies and books also work with the concept of a turning point. Sometimes it is a shift in the story that begins the resolution of a conflict. The right clue is discovered. The guy finally realizes that the girl likes him. The weakness of the aliens is at last revealed.

When my daughter McCall was younger we watched the same movies over and over again. She got on a Lion King kick for a while, and I'm sure I *heard* it a hundred times. I say *heard*, not *saw*, because most of the watching took place in our minivan while I was driving. At one point in the movie, Simba hears his dad's voice say, "Remember," and then old Rafiki hits him on the head with his stick. Simba decides to go back and claim what is his, and that was "all she wrote" for the nasty uncle, Scar. It was a turning point in the Pridelands.

JESUS IS CLOSE TO THOSE WHO ARE SUFFERING.

Just like in war, politics, sports, stories and movies, real-life turning points often represent difficult times. They can come in the form of overwhelming challenges, hardships, and even tragedies. But turning points can develop into a turn for the better, despite what the situation looks like at face value. Many times what determines whether it is a turn for the better or for the worse is not the turning point itself but rather, the way we handle it. If we hold on to God through life's challenges, we can feel Him drawing us close to Him during our time of suffering.

Isaiah 53 gives us the assurance that Jesus is close to those who are are suffering. He is well acquainted with what we're feeling when we are hurting. There is never pain without a purpose. Some of life's decisive changes come during seasons of suffering.

When we encounter Jesus, we encounter the greatest of all turning points. No one walks away from a moment with Jesus Christ without facing a change. Meeting the Savior always presents the possibility for a shift or a pivot point. When Jesus has encounters with people, He presents opportunities for life changes that can be accepted or rejected. For those who allow Jesus to turn their lives around, the divine encounters with Him are the turning points they desperately need. I believe that if we set our minds and affections on God and declare our allegiance to Jesus Christ and His perfect plan, we will find ourselves walking into a God-orchestrated turning point.

Maybe you need to experience a shift in your current situation. Perhaps you need a change in your career, your attitude, your family, or in a relationship. Maybe something from your past has come back to haunt you, and you can sense not only the need for a change, but that the change is imminent. I believe that God wants you to step into the plan that He has for you.

By the time you finish this book, I pray that you will have come face to face with Jesus Christ and His incredible, passionate love for you. He loves you more than you could ever imagine. Regardless of your situation or what you have done, He stands ready to embrace you and invite you to step into your destiny, which is the abundant life that He intended you to live.

As you read about these encounters that the Savior of the world had with people like you and me, I believe the strength and power of the One who calls each of us to a turning point will leap off of these pages and grab hold of your heart. I pray that you will have an encounter with Jesus that takes you to the point of no return—a turning point for eternity.

01
THE ORIGINAL

THE ETERNAL TURNING POINT

"Though He was God ... He made Himself nothing; He took the humble position of a slave and appeared in human form. He obediently humbled Himself even further by dying a criminal's death on a cross."

—THE APOSTLE PAUL

F aith can actually arise in your life just by reading the Bible. It's not magic; it is a fact. The Bible teaches that faith comes by hearing and hearing comes by the Word of God (Romans 10:17). When you inject the Word of God into your life, faith is a natural result. The Word of God never fades, never fails, and never changes. So as you read the following passage of Scripture, understand that something could begin to shift in your life. A pivot—a change in your life—could begin right now.

> *In the beginning was the Word, and the Word was with God, and the Word was God. He was in the beginning with God. All things were made through Him, and without Him nothing was made that was made. In Him was life, and the life was the light of men. And the light shines in the darkness, and the darkness did not comprehend it. There was a man sent from God, whose name was John. This man came for a witness, to bear witness of the Light, that all through him might believe. He was not that Light, but was sent to bear witness of that Light. That was the true Light which gives light to every man coming into the world. He was in the world, and the world was made through Him, and the world did not know Him. He came to His own, and His own did not receive Him. But as many as received Him, to them He gave the right to become children of God, to those who believe in His name: who were*

born, not of blood, nor of the will of the flesh, nor of the will of man, but of God. And the Word became flesh and dwelt among us, and we beheld His glory, the glory as of the only begotten of the Father, full of grace and truth. (John 1:1-14)

John 1 presents the Word of God as the original, eternal turning point, and we can understand this from two angles. First, there is the Word of God—the Bible. The other is the Word of God—Jesus Christ Himself.

SALVATION IS THE MAIN THEME OF THE BIBLE ... AND THE ULTIMATE TURNING POINT IN OUR LIVES.

I've heard a lot of questions about the real purpose for the Bible. "Is it a set of rules made up of do's and don'ts?" "Is it something like a charm we just place on a shelf in our homes?" "Does it give us a code or a creed?" "Is it about ordinances, churches, and denominations?" "Is it something I can beat somebody over the head with?"

In society's search for spiritual meaning, the Bible gets lumped together with the rest of the books on the subject. But the dominant message of the Bible that sets it apart from all the rest is salvation. The Word of God teaches that all have sinned and are separated from God. But it also tells us that Christ loved us so much that He died to redeem us and bring us back into relationship with Him. Salvation is the main theme of the Bible...and the ultimate turning point in our lives.

In addition, the Bible provides answers to other questions that sometimes haunt us. "Where do we go after we die?" "Is there anything else to life?" "Why do I feel alone?" "Why do I feel empty?" "Why do I have all these fears in my life?" The Bible is the map that provides the answers to all of our questions and leads us to an eternal treasure—salvation.

LIVE IN THE WORD

Because I believe all of this to be true, I also believe that we must continually live in the Word of God, consistently reading and studying it. I heard about a little girl who went to her first day of school. Her parents were excited, emotional, and anxious throughout the day. When her dad picked her up at the end of the school day, he asked her if she had learned anything. "Yeah, but I guess I didn't learn enough," she replied. "They said I have to come back again tomorrow and the next day and the next day. They told me I was gonna be here for twelve years, Daddy."

So it is with getting our spiritual education. Even with the Word of God, understanding comes little by little over a lifetime. The Bible is not just a collection of cool stories that we learn in kids' church; it is our life. Reading the Bible can be a source of strength for us. It is the instruction book for life as we know it.

I learned something about this last summer when I spent

some time in Africa. I went to Kenya and visited my friend Don Matheny and the great church he pastors in Nairobi. Then I spent a couple more weeks in South Africa, Swaziland, and Mozambique. It was very encouraging to see the opportunities that God is giving us to help so many thousands of hurting AIDS orphans.

It was a great trip, but by the time we headed home, I was exhausted. Thirty long, uncomfortable hours spent on airplanes getting home didn't allow a lot of time for catching up on rest, either. I tried to sleep but I couldn't get comfortable. Finally, my son Dylan was able to go to sleep, and I got out my Bible. I felt drawn to the gospel of John so I started reading there. From the very beginning, I began to sense God speaking to me, reminding me that He is my lifegiver. The words I was reading made me reflect on my Savior's love and grace. I felt a huge infusion of life as He spoke to me through the Bible. So, for hours on end during my trip home, I just searched the book of John. The more I read, the more clearly I saw Christ and His provision for my life, and I was strengthened by it.

The Bible does so many things for us when we read it. It cleanses us (John 15:3). It guides us, shining light on our paths (Psalm 119:105). It gives us hope. It serves as a solid foundation—a rock we can cling to.

We know that the Word of God is the Bible, but in this scripture, we can also see clearly that the Word of God is also Jesus Christ Himself. John tells us that Jesus is the Word of God in the flesh.

And the Word became flesh and dwelt among us, and we beheld His glory, the glory as of the only begotten of the Father, full of grace and truth. (John 1:14)

The Bible makes it clear that Jesus is the only Son of God. As Christians, we're adopted children of God, but there's only one Son of God. It's not like a heavenly Brady Bunch where a bunch of gods up in heaven are arguing, fighting and struggling to get along with each other. There is only one Son of God, and His name is Jesus Christ.

Jesus is the perfect man, the perfect teacher, and He is fully God all the time. If God were to look in a mirror, and you could sneak up and look over His shoulder and see His reflection, that reflection would be Jesus Christ. Jesus shows us what God is like and He is the perfect model of what God wants us to become. He wants us to be a reflection of Him to mankind.

A COMMUNITY TURNING POINT

Recently, a man who was a part of our church and a detective with the Baton Rouge Police Department was tragically killed in the line of duty during a drug raid. Our entire city was stunned. Terry Melancon's funeral was scheduled to take place at Healing Place Church, and I was given the honor of ministering in the service. I knew there would be a large crowd of people there who loved Terry—all of them hurting deeply over their loss. So much of the community wanted to show their heartfelt support for Terry's family and our law enforcement officers, the funeral soon grew into a citywide gathering. At the last minute, the decision was made to televise the funeral. This created an incredible opportunity not only to minister to Terry's family, but also to share the gospel of Jesus' love with this entire community that was hurting.

I was so nervous when I got to the church that Saturday morning that my hands would not quit shaking. I was nervous because I felt the heavy responsibility God was placing on me to minister in this situation. I thought, *I'll never be able to do this. I'll stutter and confuse my words.* I remember putting my head in my hands just prior to the funeral and crying out to God, "I can't do this." It was then that I sensed

Jesus speaking to me, saying, "That's good, Dino, *now I can do it*." Then He spoke two things to me. "Go minister to Terry's family, and don't let Me down. Don't fail Me. Present the gospel, because that's what matters when it is all said and done."

In that moment I had a turning point. I needed strength, and God provided it. He became my source of strength during a time when I wasn't sure I could handle it. Jesus showed up in those hours as we honored a hero and told about Terry's testimony for Christ. What a privilege to be part of a turning point for our whole city.

IT'S ABOUT FORGIVENESS

Jesus, the Word of God, came to earth to be the perfect sacrifice. When you think about Jesus' death on the cross, do you ever wonder why He had to go through it? Was it for our healing? Was it for our prosperity? Did He die so that we could go to church and find a spouse, or so that we could get all our bills paid? Is the cross all about making our lives better? Is it about letting us win all the time? Is Jesus some type of Santa Claus?

No, the cross can hardly be limited to an exercise in making our lives more comfortable. Certainly, God cares about our needs in this life, but the ultimate reason Jesus died on the cross is essentially for the forgiveness of sins. And if our sins are not forgiven, we have no hope.

When I was seventeen, living in Myrtle Beach, South Carolina where I grew up, I started thinking about eternity. I heard some people talking about Jesus, and I began to think, *I need to get my life right and quit staying out all weekend. There's no way I can live like this all my life.* I thought about all the things I needed to change, so I made some adjustments. I started getting really "spiritual" and tried to be a "good person."

I had been telling God for weeks what an incredibly good person I was, and how my parents were good, and how there was a church right down the street in my same zip code. That had to count for something.

I soon learned that none of those things mattered.

My real turning point came on June 21, 1982, when I realized that I had sinned, that the wages of sin is death, and that I was going to get the wages I had earned unless I turned away from my sin. I bowed my knee beside my bed, confessed my sins and prayed, "Jesus, please forgive me." Right then, there was a shift in my life. It was a pivotal moment in my life—my eternal turning point began.

The Word of God presents us with the opportunity for a turning point in our lives. Each of us must choose whether or not to confess that we're sinners in need of a Savior. When we confess, He washes away all our guilt and we experience salvation, the greatest of all turning points.

02

NICK AT NITE

THE NEW BIRTH TURNING POINT

The Christian is not one who has gone all the way with Christ. None of us has. The Christian is one who has found the right road.

—CHARLES L. ALLEN
(1913-2005, NOTABLE METHODIST MINISTER)

Some turning points have immediate impact on your life. Others take some time before you can really understand what has happened. Sometimes we make decisions that seem trivial or insignificant at the time, but they end up shaping our lives from that point forward.

DECISIONS ARE LIKE SMALL HINGES THAT ALLOW BIG DOORS TO SWING IN YOUR LIFE.

Many times decisions are like small hinges that allow big doors to swing in our lives. Making the decision to ask DeLynn to marry me turned out to be one of the best decisions I ever made. The most important was my decision to be a fully committed follower of Christ. When I look back, there's no way I understood at the time how dramatically those two decisions would shape my life.

A QUEST FOR TRUTH

I believe this is what happened to Nicodemus. He had no idea the enormity of the turning point he was heading into when he set out to see Jesus one night. That's why I call it the Nick-at-Nite turning point.

In John 3 we get a little snapshot of Nicodemus' encounter with Jesus Christ. It's a great story about an individual who meets Jesus, realizes that what he has is not enough, and receives an invitation to become a fully committed follower of Christ.

Nicodemus needs a turning point. His life needs a twist. In the following verses, it's amazing to see how this need in Nicodemus' life—this desire to receive something more—comes to the surface. Nicodemus comes face to face with Truth.

> *There was a man of the Pharisees named Nicodemus, a ruler of the Jews. This man came to Jesus by night and said to Him, "Rabbi, we know that You are a teacher come from God; for no one can do these signs that You do unless God is with him." Jesus answered and said to him, "Most assuredly, I say to you, unless one is born again, he cannot see the kingdom of God." Nicodemus said to Him, "How can a man be born when he is old? Can he enter a second time into his mother's womb and be born?" (John 3:1-4)*

Nicodemus is puzzled. Jesus can tell that his mind is spinning, so He continues:

> *Jesus answered, "Most assuredly, I say to you, unless one is born of water and the Spirit, he cannot enter the kingdom of God. That which is born of the flesh is flesh, and that which is born of the Spirit is spirit. Do not marvel that I said to you, 'You must be born again.' The wind blows where it wishes, and you hear the sound of it, but cannot tell where it comes from and where it goes. So*

> is everyone who is born of the Spirit." *Nicodemus*
> *answered and said to Him, "How can these things*
> *be?" (John 3:5-9)*

I love Nicodemus' response as Jesus tries to help him understand the fullness of life God intends for mankind. Nicodemus says to Him, "How can these things be? I'm not getting it. I'm hearing You, but I'm not seeing it."

Jesus is trying to explain His heart's cry. Nicodemus is trying to understand, but he is just not getting it. It can be really frustrating to be trying your best to explain something to someone, but no matter how hard you try, they just sit there looking at you with eyes glazed over.

So what does Jesus do? Does He slam the door in Nicodemus' face? Hardly. Nor does He tell Nicodemus, "Well, I'll tell you what you need to do. Study up on this and go do a bunch of good deeds, and then you can come back and speak to Me. You haven't done enough and you don't understand enough on your own yet."

SIN WILL MESS UP EVERYTHING. IT WILL PARALYZE YOU. IT WILL DESTROY YOUR LIFE.

Jesus actually *wants* Nicodemus to get it. It is such a relief to me to know that Jesus wants him to understand His heart. It tells me that He really wants us to understand it today, too. He will go to great lengths to make sure we understand His plan for us. He doesn't want us to wander aimlessly in a maze of thoughts about life, wondering why we are here, how to find peace, and what happens after we die. No, not at all. Not then for Nicodemus, and not now for us.

So Jesus says to Nicodemus, "Okay, let Me break it down for you. It's like Moses. You remember Moses, Nicodemus?"

Nicodemus perks up a bit. He leans in a little closer to Jesus. "Yeah, yeah. I remember him; keep talking."

"Do you remember how Moses lifted up the serpent in the wilderness?"

"Ah, yeah, yeah, I'm following You. I know that story." Nicodemus is starting to feel the connection. Jesus reminds him about the Old Testament account of some of disobedient Israelites. Because of their sin, snakes came into the camp and bit everybody, and they were all dying. So Moses put a graven image of a snake up on a stick, lifted it up, and everybody who looked at it was saved from the bites of the snakes. It is an actual story that can be found in Numbers 21:7-9.

Jesus asks Nicodemus, "Do you know how that works?"

"Oh, sure. I'm clear on it. I understand that. I remember as a young boy training to be a rabbi. I studied that story, but how does it relate to You and me now?"

Jesus goes on to explain, "The same thing applies here, Nick. Just like that, I must be lifted up because I am the only One who will rescue you from the deadly bite of sin."

Jesus taught Nicodemus that sin has a deadly, deadly bite.

Sin will mess up everything. It will paralyze you. It will destroy your life.

Sin will even mess up the lives of other people who are around you. Arrogance and pride will do that. Greed and lust will do that. Stealing and lying will do that. It will spread like venom. It's like poison. And Jesus said, "I am the only One who can help your sin problem. If you will look to Me, I can save you from the poison of unbelief and doubt."

I'm reminded of the times in my own life when I was so self-centered and self-absorbed that sin slithered in and bit me. Oh, the pain! And I'm reminded of the collateral damage to others. We've all been there.

And then there's John 3:16. The entire gospel is summed up in these twenty-five words:

> *For God so loved the world that He gave His only begotten Son that whoever believes in Him should not perish, but have everlasting life. For God did not send His Son into the world to condemn the world, but that the world through Him might be saved. He who believes in Him is not condemned. But he who does not believe is condemned already, because he has not believed in the name of the only begotten Son of God. This is the condemnation. Light has come into the world. Men loved darkness rather than light because their deeds were evil. (John 3:16-19)*

I can see Jesus putting His hand on Nicodemus's shoulder. "Watch this, Nicodemus. Get this."

> *Everyone practicing evil hates the light and does not come to the light, lest his deeds would be exposed. But he who does truth comes to the light, that his deeds may be clearly seen that they have been done in God. (John 3:20, 21)*

I just love this story. I used to read this story and get down on Nicodemus, but now I read it with a whole new level of compassion. Think about how many people didn't go to see Jesus because they were afraid what people would say.

I have tried to imagine what was going on that made Nicodemus decide to visit Jesus that night. He had vast knowledge—years of education and experience. He had a strong background. He had years of history in the religious world. But despite all of those things, something happened to make him realize that what he had on the inside was no longer adequately answering his questions and meeting his needs. It wasn't working, so he went to see Jesus.

Imagine if he told some of his friends that he was thinking about going to see Jesus. "I've been listening to Him. I watched Him the other day and was amazed at how He handled people. I watched Him reach out to the blind, and I saw Him feed people. I listened to His words, and I've never heard anything like it. I think God may have sent Him, so I think I'm going to go talk to Him about some spiritual thoughts."

Can you hear his friends' reaction? "What?! Why would you want to do that? Remember who you are. You're an educated and trained leader. If there's anybody who has a lock on spiritual stuff and deserves to be chief in the kingdom, it's you. You have the background and the upbringing, and that's all you need. Don't risk all of it by getting mixed up with that crowd."

I STILL HAVEN'T FOUND WHAT I'M LOOKING FOR

But Nicodemus said, "Thanks for the compliments, but what you don't understand is that I still have something missing in my soul." He was a spiritual man who had learned a lot, but there was still a void in his life. Nicodemus had a hunger to know more. He was ready to quit depending on spiritual hand-me-downs and investigate Jesus for himself.

As you look at your own life, maybe you see you're like Nicodemus. Think about your background, your tradition, your doctrine, your theology, your parents' faith, your grandparents' faith, and your upbringing. When all of that no longer answers the deepest need of your heart, you have a faith crisis. The things that have been propping you up no longer prop you up. Things start to slip a little ... then a lot.

Then you start wondering, "Why am I here, anyway? What is my purpose in life?" When you have a faith crisis, you want to talk to somebody you can trust. You don't want to talk to a phony because that's just nauseating. You don't want somebody who can talk about it, but doesn't bother to live it. You don't want to talk to anybody who is a hypocrite—who talks one way but lives another. At that point in your life, you want to find somebody that you can trust with the deepest needs of your heart.

Nicodemus was in a faith crisis, and when he looked at Jesus, he saw someone he could trust. Jesus gave him all the answers that he had been searching for. He gave Nicodemus a clear view of the truth about God's plan for his life.

Jesus shot straight with Nicodemus. "You know what? I know this is going to be hard to understand because of the mindset you've had all of your life, but here's the truth. No one is good enough to go to heaven. I know you've worked on a scale system, thinking that if you do enough good to outweigh the bad, you will get into the kingdom of God. But that's not the truth. If you aren't forgiven, you cannot go to heaven. The issue is that you must be born from above. You must look to Me. As a matter of fact, Nicodemus, I'm glad that you believe I have been sent from God, but recognizing that I've been sent from God is not enough. You must recognize Me as the only Son of God. That is an important distinction."

THE TRUTH IS THAT GOD CAN CHANGE ANYONE.

Jesus told Nicodemus all these things, carefully breaking everything down for him. He told him about the importance of having a personal relationship with God rather than a relationship based on his heritage, stressing that the only entrance into the kingdom of God is through individual repentance and rebirth.

I love what Nicodemus did during this conversation. He just sat there listening and letting his coffee get cold. He thought, *Whoa! This is not at all what I thought.* As Jesus continued to unpack more truth, Nicodemus sat on the edge of his seat. Somewhere in the back of his mind, he was thinking, *Wow! They never taught anything like this in seminary.*

God can touch people we think are unreachable. The truth is that He can change anyone.

Jesus made His point very clear to Nicodemus. "What I'm looking for is heart knowledge, not head knowledge." Head knowledge is good, but you must understand that your head knowledge will not save you. In spiritual matters, God is looking for heart knowledge.

Think about that. God does not want just your mind—He wants your heart. When I asked DeLynn to marry me, I didn't go to her and say, "Baby, I really love you intellectually. Brain to brain, I'm all about you. Here, baby, I want to give you my brain. I love you with all my intellect." DeLynn did not want my brain. She wanted my heart, because it's the heart that matters most, and she knew if she had my heart, the rest of me would follow.

God's incredible patience is shown in the story of Nicodemus' encounter with Jesus. Even though it takes time for some people to understand God's plan for them, God never gives up. God is patient with sincere seekers, and He's also very persistent because He knows that eternal destinies are at stake—the timer is ticking away in our lives, and eventually, when it stops ticking, it will be heaven or hell.

I became aware of this truth one night when I woke up hungry and decided to sneak a bowl of cereal. I went on a prowl in the kitchen at about 2:30 a.m. I grabbed some Peanut Butter Crunch, and pulled out a big Tupperware® bowl. I didn't use one of those little china dishes. No real man eats out of a glass bowl after two in the morning. You get "big plastic" and pour in half a box of cereal and grab a giant serving spoon.

ETERNAL DESTINIES ARE AT STAKE—THE TIMER IS TICKING AWAY IN OUR LIVES, AND WHEN IT STOPS TICKING, IT WILL BE HEAVEN OR HELL.

I stepped back for a second to survey the scene, and it touched me. I sighed—quietly but sincerely, "Ahhh." All I needed was the milk, so I went to the fridge, opened the door, reached in, and found the gallon of vitamin D. As I pulled out the half-full carton, I saw something that made me weep. The expiration date was a week old. It broke my heart.

I'll never forget that night, not so much because of the heartbreak I felt over the milk, but because of what happened next. As I tried to eat that huge Tupperware® bowl full of dry Peanut Butter Crunch, I sensed the Holy Spirit saying to me, "Son, just like every gallon of milk has an expiration date, every single person has an expiration date. Every time you look into someone's eyes, realize that there is an expiration date on that person. The bad news is that they don't know the date, but the good news is that they don't have to expire alone. You need to tell them to live ready."

Our merciful God is persistent yet patient with those who sincerely seek Him. He was patient as Nicodemus struggled to understand, and I'm glad that He was patient with me as I sought my own turning point and finally turned my life over to Him.

You can see how the life of Nicodemus was impacted by his encounter with Jesus. Later in the book of John, we see him with all of his peers—the Pharisees, Sadducees, and all the Sanhedrin—and he is speaking up for Jesus. It was a scenario that would not be very good for his career. But he spoke up because they were plotting to assassinate Jesus (John 7:50, 51).

JESUS NEVER TURNS AWAY ANYONE WHO IS SINCERELY SEEKING A TURNING POINT.

Later, in John 19:39, Nicodemus shows up by the cross, and again he's standing up for Christ. He's helping the others take Jesus' body off of the cross and preparing Him for burial.

This story shows us that God can use anyone. Who would have thought that Nicodemus would show up Passion Week as an ally? He came back on the scene as someone committed to following Jesus Christ. I would have never thought that, but that's how the plan of God works. No matter who you are, God can do amazing things in your life if you'll let Him.

Maybe you're like I was when I realized that my tradition and my limited knowledge and theology were of very little significance. The things I had learned from my parents and what I understood about church were no longer enough to touch my deepest need. I had a spiritual faith crisis because my life was not lining up with the Word of God. My hand-me-down faith was not doing the job.

So, I did what Nicodemus did. I turned to Christ because I felt like He was someone I could trust. When I looked at His life, I thought, *Now, that's someone who is not phony.*

Maybe you feel the same way. My advice to you is to do what Nicodemus did. Go to Christ. Jesus never turns away anyone who is seeking for a turning point. You may be totally surprised when you look back over your life in years to come—this could be the most important decision of your life.

03

THAT'S NOT WHAT I ORDERED

A TURNING POINT IN FAITH AND OBEDIENCE

Faith is deliberate confidence in the character of God whose ways you may not understand at the time.

—OSWALD CHAMBERS (1874-1917, SCOTTISH PREACHER)

So Jesus came again to Cana of Galilee where He had made the water wine. And there was a certain nobleman whose son was sick at Capernaum. When he heard that Jesus had come out of Judea into Galilee, he went to Him and implored Him to come down and heal his son, for he was at the point of death. Then Jesus said to him, "Unless you people see signs and wonders, you will by no means believe." The nobleman said to Him, "Sir, come down before my child dies!" Jesus said to him, "Go your way; your son lives." So the man believed the word that Jesus spoke to him, and he went his way. And as he was now going down, his servants met him and told him, saying, "Your son lives!" Then he inquired of them the hour when he got better. And they said to him, "Yesterday at the seventh hour the fever left him." So the father knew that it was at the same hour in which Jesus said to him, "Your son lives." And he himself believed, and his whole household. (John 4:46-53)

This is a story about a turning point in the life of a royal official. He was living the good life. He had a wife and son, a great job, plenty of influence in the community and money in the bank, and things were going well. Other people were struggling, but he wasn't.

Then something happened that started a meltdown in his life. All of a sudden his precious son got a fever, and the fever wouldn't break. Although he and his wife were doing everything they could to help their son get better, he kept getting worse. They had clout, money, and privilege, but none of those things could cure their boy. The boy's body was melting away from the fever, and his parents didn't know what else to do.

Sometimes you can't have a plan for everything. Sometimes things happen and catch you off guard. Even in the reality of our faith and knowing that Jesus is our Lord, some things happen that come as a surprise to us.

WHAT DO YOU DO WHEN THE ANSWER YOU GET IS NOT WHAT YOU EXPECT?

I've been with parents who had a child in the hospital, and no one had an answer for the situation. I have sat with moms and dads who told me, "We don't know what's going to happen. The doctors don't really know what to do." Maybe you have had a child with an illness that baffled the doctors. And because they couldn't find a solution, all you could do was wait and see. Those are the times when your heart begins to ache, and as you are "waiting and seeing," your child is getting worse.

This was the scene in the home of this royal official. Having exhausted all his resources, this distraught father started

CHAPTER THREE

asking anyone and everyone for ideas. And that's when someone told him about a man who had been healing the sick.

Maybe it was one of his servants who spoke up and said, "Sir, I've got an idea. There's a man in Cana named Jesus. People say He's a miracle worker. He lays hands on people and they're healed. Maybe you need to find Him and ask Him to come here."

IN PURSUIT OF THE MIRACLE WORKER

That father didn't waste a moment but set out immediately to find Jesus. And the Bible says he went on a twenty-mile trip that took him to Cana. When he got there, he began asking everyone, "Where is Jesus? Have you heard of this Jesus, the miracle worker?"

Finally, someone pointed him to a big crowd of people. "He's been teaching here for two or three days now, and you wouldn't believe the things that are happening. You've got to see it."

People had gathered around, trying to see what Jesus was going to do next—as if He were a sideshow at the circus. When the father got there, a buzz of excitement was in the crowd.

The sick boy's father interrupted the scene. He pushed right through the crowd and said, "Jesus! Jesus! Sir, please, please, my son is sick to the point of death. I'm from Capernaum, and I need You to come back with me. It's twenty miles away, but I'll take care of everything. I just need You to come to my house with me and lay hands on my son who is dying."

After hearing this desperate plea, Jesus did something that seems a little odd. He said something that I wouldn't have expected Him to say. Jesus looked around at the crowd that was witnessing this encounter and said to them, "Do I have to do miraculous signs and wonders before you will believe me?" (John 4:48).

To me, that seems like an odd response. But as Jesus looked around and realized that the crowd had an excessive appetite for excitement, He determined that He would not allow His signs, wonders and miracles to become a circus sideshow. Just imagine it: "Come one. Come all. See the carpenter now turned miracle worker." Never! Jesus would never let that happen.

He looked at the crowds and said, "You are coming after Me because of the sensationalism, and that's not what this is all about." Then He turned to the desperate father and said, "I'm going to help you, sir, but I'm not going to do it the way you expect Me to."

The royal official pleaded and begged, "Lord, please come now before my little boy dies." It was as though he had not heard what Jesus said. He continued begging, "Can You please come and help me now? My son is dying." In his desperation he couldn't understand what Jesus was saying. He didn't have time to talk, he just needed Jesus to stick to the formula and come with him. He wasn't accustomed to begging, but he had nothing left to surrender except his dignity.

In his eyes, this was a desperate situation and he needed immediate help, and he was willing to do anything for it.

Then Jesus said to him, "Go back home. Your son will live."

What do you do when the answer you get is not what you expect? You are facing a turning point—a decisive moment. Something significant can take place right here.

DECISION TIME

This desperate father was standing at a turning point of faith and obedience. Jesus had told him to go home and his son would live. Now he must decide whether or not to believe Jesus. The dilemma churned in his mind. *This isn't how it is supposed to work. Should I just believe Him and go home? Or should I keep begging Him to come with me?*

What a decision! What would you have done if you had been in this father's shoes?

OVERCOMING OBSTACLES REQUIRES FAITH AND OBEDIENCE.

The man stepped away from Jesus, took a deep breath, and began the journey home alone—without Jesus. He decided to take Jesus at His word and he started off on the twenty-mile journey home. As the parent of a critically ill child—a father who had decided to believe the words of Jesus—those twenty miles in that situation must have seemed like two hundred miles. But he moved ahead in total obedience and with amazing faith.

That's not the end of the story, though. The Bible tells us that while he was on his way, some of his servants met him with the news that his son was alive and well. He asked them when the boy had begun to feel better, and they replied, "Yesterday afternoon at one o'clock, his fever suddenly disappeared."

They said, "We don't know what happened. Your son was melting away, and we had given up all hope since we had not heard from you. But then all of a sudden the fever broke." Then the Bible says that the officer and his entire household believed in Jesus.

NOT JUST A LAST RESORT

One of the most important things this story teaches us is to go to Jesus with our needs. And don't go to Him just as a last resort. He loves us and is always available to meet our needs, so go to Him first. I Peter 5:7 says that we can cast all our care upon Him, because He cares for us. So why not go to Him from the beginning?

This royal official had to humble himself. He needed more than what his possessions and status could do for him. So he traveled a long distance to see if Jesus would come to his home and heal his son. But when things didn't happen the way he had planned, he submitted to the words of Jesus. Because of his faith and obedience, his son was healed. This hurting father didn't let arrogance rule the day.

GOD IS ALWAYS MORE CONCERNED ABOUT YOUR HEART THAN THE MIRACLE.

I think this story also lets us see that we should be ready for obstacles. When you step out to get your needs met, you must be ready to face obstacles. And to get through the obstacles, you must take steps of faith and obedience. The father in this story was a man who refused to allow any obstacle to stop him, even if it meant sticking his neck out and risking his pride. Even though it didn't come the way he ordered it, he got his answer. It came with an obstacle that required him to take a step of faith.

This is the same kind of faith and determination we all need, because a faith that requires no effort is a faith that is not very effective. We will all be faced with obstacles in life, and it will take determination to overcome them.

I love Tom Landry, the coach of the Dallas Cowboys back when they won their first Super Bowl. He made this interesting statement about determination: "The job of a coach is to challenge the team to do what they do not want to do in order to achieve what they've always wanted."

The father didn't want to head home without Jesus. But he was determined to get what he wanted even though it meant doing things a different way. God answered this man's prayer, but not exactly the way he asked Him to do it. When faced with the obstacle of not getting what he wanted as ordered, this man decided to go with God's plan—a very wise decision.

God is not the Sonic girl on roller skates asking, "Do you need some cheese with your tater tots?" Sometimes we don't get what we order. We simply need to learn to take Jesus at His word.

The bottom line is that God is always more concerned about your heart than the miracle. We put in our order for deliverance, but God wants to develop our character, integrity, and honesty. We order miracles, but God gives us truth. We order signs, but He wants us to have sincerity. We order hype, but He wants to give us humility. And we say, "God, that's not what I ordered." But if we're wise, like the desperate father we will follow God's plan, and enjoy the good results.

This story ends with the man back at home, holding his healthy son in his arms, and his entire household joining him in believing in the Son of God.

It is liberating when we realize that God is in control and we are not. Acknowledging that God knows more than we do brings a real sense of freedom that allows us to trust Him more and more.

Everyone goes through difficult turning points. But when things are not going the way you expected, you face a choice: Will you get *bitter* or *better*? You can fight against God, demand your own way, and get bitter. Or, like the royal official, you can obey Jesus, take Him at His word, and get better. It's up to you.

A BEACHSIDE TURNING POINT

When my father passed away seventeen years ago, it was a very tough time for me. My dad was a good old strong Italian man who liked to take care of his family. He was the godfather of the Rizzo family. He handled everything for us. He sent me to Bible College, paid for the honeymoon for DeLynn and me, and bought us our first sofa. He was a giver to the max.

Then he had a brain aneurysm, and in a few short minutes, fell into a coma, and was put in the hospital where we stayed forty-five days. During those days, I watched my dad wither away to about ninety-five pounds, never moving, never responding. This strong, Italian man who had delighted in taking care of the Rizzo family, was now unresponsive in a hospital bed. It was almost more than I could handle.

THE LORD SAID, "SON, CAN YOU TRUST ME IN THE MIDDLE OF THE MYSTERY?"

We asked everyone we knew to come to the hospital, and we prayed for him together. I spent hours and hours beside his bed, praying for him and reading the Bible to him.

Well-meaning people offered various opinions about why he wasn't healed. One night someone told me, "God says that if you will stay up all night and read the Scripture to him, he will get out of that bed in the morning." Guess what I did. I stayed up all night and read the Scripture to him. But he didn't get out of bed the next morning. He died five days later.

It was a critical moment in my life. And to be honest, I really felt ripped off, and I got angry. I thought, *Here I am running buses into the inner city, leading Bible studies in my home, going into high schools to reach young people, and doing what I can to teach people about God's love. And yet, He can't even work up a little miracle for me?* I started blaming people, and my blame turned into bitterness.

I returned to Myrtle Beach about three months after my father died, and I stood on the beach at about four o'clock in the morning, crying out to God. I was complaining, complaining, complaining. Then the Lord just dropped something into my heart. It wasn't an audible voice. The Lord just spoke to my heart and said, "Son, you are going to have to make a decision tonight. You're going to have to deal with this before we can go any further. We're going to have to end this whole thing right here until you realize that I have never made one mistake, and that I'm always right and have never done anything wrong. Can you trust Me even though you don't understand Me? Can you trust Me in the middle of the mystery? Will you decide to trust Me no matter what? If we can't cross this bridge, we can't go any further."

Standing there on the beach, I took a deep breath and said, "Lord, even though I can't see You, even though I can't feel You, even though right now I'm not sure I understand this, I'm making the decision to trust You. I choose to believe that You are right, that You have never been wrong, and that You are in control and I am not."

I cannot describe the freedom that turning point brought to my life. Do I have it all figured out now? No. I'm a stratosphere away from that. But no matter what comes my way or how crazy things may get, it helps me to know that God is in control and I'm not. He is always right, and I'm going to trust Him.

There will be times when you'll face turning points that you won't understand. Sometimes God will answer your prayer, but not the way you "ordered." He will answer your prayer, but it will be on His terms. Don't get bitter, don't blame God, and don't run away. Instead, determine to trust Him and obey Him regardless of the situation. Find the freedom of not having to be in control. Find the turning point of trust.

4

THE OTHER SIDE OF THE STORM

CROSSING OVER TO A TURNING POINT

O LORD, how long will You forget me?
  – Forever?
How long will You look the other way?
How long must I struggle with anguish in my soul,
With sorrow in my heart every day?

— DAVID, KING OF ISRAEL (1010-970 BC)

Turning points can freak us out. Have you ever been in a situation that just scared the daylights out of you? I'm talking about the type of fear that makes you unable to breathe and starts making red splotches come up on your neck.

I visited Ron Luce at the Teen Mania campus in Texas with a few friends earlier this year. As part of the "experience," Ron had us all try out some of the activities they have set up there for the teenagers they work with. He wanted me to do the ropes course, which included a ride down a zip line that was about seventy-five feet in the air across some woods.

I was terrified. I was too old, too big, and too scared. As I climbed up to the platform, I got real spiritual. I made promises to God and repented of all my sin. I repented of *any* sin, for that matter, whether I'd done it or not.

GOD WANTS TO SHOW US THAT THERE IS ALWAYS ANOTHER SIDE TO WHATEVER WE'RE GOING THROUGH.

Stepping off that platform was a turning point for me. I got totally freaked out, but by the time it was all over, I was exhilarated. I made it to the other side and finished the course alive.

Sometimes we act like life is one-sided. We only see one side of the battle we're fighting. We only see one side of our obstacles, but God wants to show us that there is always another side to whatever we're going through.

Jesus was always asking His disciples to follow Him. He often led them to breakthrough situations that brought them to new levels of obedience and faith in their lives. He would bring them along, and sometimes they would get scared and act as if they weren't sure if they could go that far. But then He would nudge them to a place closer to the edge of their faith.

Luke 8 relates one of these encounters that Jesus had with His disciples:

> Now it happened, on a certain day, that He got into a boat with His disciples. And He said to them, "Let us cross over to the other side of the lake." And they launched out. But as they sailed He fell asleep. And a windstorm came down on the lake, and they were filling with water, and were in jeopardy. And they came to Him and awoke Him, saying, "Master, Master, we are perishing!" Then He arose and rebuked the wind and the raging of the water. And they ceased, and there was a calm. But He said to them, "Where is your faith?" And they were afraid, and marveled, saying to one another, "Who can this be? For He commands even the winds and water, and they obey Him!" (Luke 8:22-25)

There was something on the other side of the lake that made Jesus want to leave the side of the lake He was on, and take a twenty-mile boat ride. What was it that was drawing Jesus to the other side?

It turns out that it wasn't *what* was on the other side but *who* was on the other side. There was somebody on the other side who was hurting, helpless, and hopeless. The Bible tells us that this "somebody" was a maniac. He was a desperate individual, a pitiful soul that was full of the devil. Evil was ravaging his life. He lived in a cemetery, and the Bible says that he even cut himself with stones. He hated his life, and he hated everybody else. The devil had full control of him.

Jesus wanted to cross the lake because there was a life to be liberated on the other side. There was someone to serve. Throughout the New Testament, if you find someone helpless, hopeless, and hurting, you usually find Jesus close by. He's a Savior who searches for people who have been left out or abandoned.

IT'S TIME FOR A NAP

He loaded up all of His disciples in the boat, and they launched out to find this hopeless man. Once the trip was underway, Jesus went to the back and took a nap.

We all know that naps can sneak up on us. Sometimes I'll get in that certain comfortable position, and in five minutes I'm asleep. If I sit still long enough, I'm going to sleep. I can go to sleep just about anywhere and at anytime.

I was counseling with a lady in my office a while back,

and she was pouring out her heart to me—just unpacking all of it. It was about two o'clock—right after lunch—and I had been to a Chinese buffet and packed it in. And it was about 100 degrees in my office. I was listening and trying really hard to concentrate, but before long, I was tossing out some z's. The next thing I knew, the lady was saying, "Pastor! Pastor! You were sleeping!"

"No, ma'am. I was praying for you." She knew better, and I confessed, but I still felt so bad. I felt like a dog, and I thought, "I've got to get out of ministry. It's over."

But she was so cool about it. "Oh, pastor. You're just so crazy. You're the craziest pastor in the world." Then she just kept right on talking. She didn't miss a beat.

I don't think Jesus fell asleep accidentally, though. I think He took a nap because He was tired, and was not concerned about the storm that was coming. He knew where they were going and He knew He needed to rest.

I think it is a very interesting snapshot of Jesus. The Son of God was snoozing in the back of the boat. This is the One of whom John spoke, saying, "Behold! The Lamb of God who takes away the sin of the world!" (John 1:29). God Almighty, the Savior of the world, was taking a nap. It is an amazing picture of our Savior's humanness.

While Jesus was asleep, I have no doubt that all of the disciples were very much awake. Their minds had to be reeling with excitement over the adventure they had just been on with Jesus. A widow's son had been raised from the dead, a centurion's servant had been healed, and many, many others had been cured of their sicknesses. It had been something incredible to witness, and they were riding high when they set out on the trip.

In my family, it always seems like at the beginning of a trip everything is always so cool. I'm sure it is that way for all of us. In the interest of having some nice, quality time with the family, you decide to drive across the country instead of fly. So you load everyone up in the SUV, put on a DVD for the kids, and get out the beef jerky. Maybe you even start to sing a few songs. "This land is your land, this land is my land...." You're on a family road trip and everything feels really great.

But before you get two hours away from home, everyone is upset, you're fussing at the kids, the DVD is skipping, no one remembers the words to the songs, and you're out of beef jerky!

Trips can start off great, but sometimes they don't stay that way. Difficulties arise and you are faced with challenges in your journey. In the same way, if you're going to follow Jesus and walk the walk of faith, eventually you'll encounter some hurdles. There are going to be moments when you have to row against the tide.

That's what happened to the disciples. Jesus was sleeping in the back of the boat, and suddenly a storm popped up. Why is it that when we make a commitment to our family, to church, to give, to pray, or to live right, all of a sudden, right on cue, there is an obstacle?

Maybe you have said to yourself, "I'm going to get up

early in the morning. My wife and I are going to pray, and we're going to start reading the Bible. We're going to spend more time together, and we're not going to continue to live the way we're living now." Why is it that right then, seemingly out of nowhere, a problem pops up?

It happened to the disciples on this journey. The storm showed up right on cue. The devil knew that if he could stop the boat, he could keep that man on the other side bound up. Not only that, but if Jesus didn't get to the other side of the lake, any good that the man could do would be stopped. If you read ahead in the story, the Bible tells us that after his turning point, this man—this maniac–turned-missionary—started going to his family and into the ten-city region nearby to tell people about Jesus. So, the devil wanted to stop the boat from crossing over because he knew that in a few short hours he would lose an essential weapon in keeping that community bound up in fear. Certainly he was going to try to mess up the trip. It is the same thing he does to us today. Every time we make a decision to begin serving God with a greater passion, he will try to brew up a storm to stop us.

When the storm comes, it screams at us, "Quit believing. Quit giving. Quit sending. Quit trusting. Quit sacrificing." It blows gusts of fear at us, and all too often, we start thinking that we may not be able to make it.

GOD IS IN CONTROL—EVEN IN THE MIDST OF YOUR STORMS.

I'm not a real good boat buddy. If I go on a boat with you, I *will* vomit on you before the end of the day. That's what I do in a boat. I vomit. Some guys feel real comfortable in a boat, but I'm a wreck the whole time. I load up on medicine for seasickness, I wear my life jacket the whole time, and every time the boat rocks, I think we're starting to sink.

But the disciples were good at boating. They understood the ins and outs of their boat. They had been through at least a hundred storms before. Yet, when this storm began, they started panicking. These expert boatmen thought they were sinking. The Bible says they scrambled over to Jesus and woke Him up, shouting, "Master, we are drowning! We're all about to die!" They thought that because they were in the middle of a storm, God had lost control. "Jesus, this is really bad. We've lost our bearings. We're all drenched and worn out, and we can't hang on any longer. Everybody's getting sick. We're not going to make it."

A lot of times we will start doubting in the dark what God gave us in the light. We forget our mission. We forget our focus, and we lose sight of what God has promised. We lose sight of the promises of God and start thinking about our immediate needs. We start asking, "What about me? What am I supposed to do? My needs are not being met. Has anyone thought about my needs? What about today? What about this week? I'm worn out and I can't take much more." We start thinking that we're sinking... drowning... perishing. "It's so bad. I'm hurt so bad. I'm so disappointed. Jesus, don't You care about me? I'm drowning."

When they woke Jesus up, for some reason Jesus didn't join in their panic. He said, "Whoa, whoa, whoa! You're not perishing. You're in a storm. And there is a big difference. This is a storm. This is rain. This is motion."

But here's the clincher: Jesus said to them, *"You're* not perishing. The guy on the other side of this lake—*he* is perishing. He's lost his home and his family, and nobody cares about him. He does not have Me in his boat, and he is perishing."

Sometimes we get in a struggle, and we begin to think that God has abandoned us. We forget that Jesus is in the boat with us. Our memory of the promises He has given us grows dim, and we make the situation seem worse than it is. Honestly, how bad can it be? If Jesus is your Savior, you are going to heaven. You're not going to hell. How bad can it really be for anyone who has the hope of heaven? There are storms that are legitimately rough and terrible, but remember this: there's a huge difference between going through a storm and perishing.

THERE'S A HUGE DIFFERENCE BETWEEN GOING THROUGH A STORM AND PERISHING.

The Bible shows us that Jesus wasn't very sympathetic with the disciples, either. I love how He just looked at them and said to the storm, "Shhh. Peace be still." Maybe the disciples thought He was talking to them. Either way, it worked for them as well as for the waves.

"Shhh." He calmed it all. Then He looked at His disciples who were worn out, drenched head–to-toe, and still a little green from being seasick. But now their jaws were dropped and they were stunned and relieved all at the same time.

A LESSON ABOUT FAITH

Jesus looked at these men He loved so much and asked them, "Where is your faith? Why haven't you learned to trust Me?"

Think about it. How often do we get in the middle of

something and then trouble hits? We start making assessments and conclude that we're dying. It's all over; we're through; we are finished. But Jesus says to us, "Where is your faith? This isn't the other side of the lake yet. Is this the promise that I gave you? Is this what My Word has given to you? No, this is the middle of the lake. You're not dying in the middle of it. *I'm* certainly not going out this way. You are going to the other side because *I am in your boat.* Would you please trust that I have everything under control and that I'm going to get you through this?"

When Jesus is in the boat—when He is in your heart, and you trust Him as your Savior—He will get you to the other side. No matter what you're going through right now, there is another side to it. No matter what you're facing, God will help you get to the other side of it.

Maybe it's depression, defeat, doubt, or discouragement. Whatever it is, don't start thinking that it is the end of it all. Remember, there's another side to defeat. There's another side to your past. There's another side to the sickness that you're fighting right now. There's another side to a troubled marriage. You have to decide that you are going to hold on until you get to the other side. Jesus is in your boat, and you're not going down.

Jesus didn't give you the dream of getting to the other side only to abandon you in a storm when you're halfway there. And remember this: your turning point is not just for you. On the shoreline of your breakthrough, there are people who are in need of hope and healing.

05

WHERE ARE THEY NOW?

A PERSONAL TURNING POINT

Forgiveness breaks the cycle of blame and loosens the stranglehold of guilt. It accomplishes these two things through a remarkable linkage, placing the forgiver on the same side as the party who did the wrong.

—PHILIP YANCEY (AUTHOR)

When we read the Bible, we can look ahead and check out the end of the story. But I often try to put myself in some of the scenes the Bible describes, and it's difficult to try to comprehend the tension of an encounter like this one, and not yet know how the story will end.

We can look at the story of the woman caught in adultery in John 8 and see one of the greatest turning points of all time. It is probably one of my own favorites, but then again, I love all the close-encounter turning points between Christ and a lost soul.

Imagine how the woman in this story would later tell it:

As they brought me to Jesus, our eyes met and there was something there that I had never seen before, and I really couldn't put my finger on it. You see, they brought me to Him to try to trap Him; to try to get Him to say something against the law. You know, looking back, I don't think there is anything anyone could have ever done or said to catch Him in any sin, but I was caught.

Those Pharisees had caught me in the very act of my sin. They caught me red-handed in an adulterous affair with a married man. I felt so dirty and so ugly as they dragged me through the city to the temple. I feared my punishment because I knew what was awaiting me. I knew that the written law said any woman like me was to be stoned to death at the city gates.

Do you have any idea what it's like to be categorized as such a woman? The shame and guilt I felt that day were indescribable. Everyone's eyes just glared at me in disgust and judgment. As they threw me down in front of Jesus, I wondered if He too would judge me; if He too would condemn me.

The Pharisees asked Jesus what He thought they should do to me. My stomach knotted up and tears came to my eyes because I was sure that my judgment was on its way. That's when He looked at me. I'll never forget that look. Rather than judgment, His response was silence. He bent down and started writing something in the sand with His finger. I'm not sure what He wrote. But after what seemed like an eternity, He looked at me as He said to my accusers, "Those without sin, stone her first."

I braced myself. But after a few moments, I started to hear stones falling to the ground one by one. The stones that were judgment to carry out my execution were the same stones that had exposed their sin. One by one, those Pharisees walked away. They walked away leaving me all alone with Him.

I was broken, confused, unspeakably relieved, and wondering what just happened. I didn't know what to say or do; I didn't even know what to think. I had heard that some people had called Him the Son of God—the Messiah. I, too, had witnessed Him healing some sick people. And now He had done something for me.

I realized that I had encountered the Christ, not just some other man waiting to heap His religious condemnation on me. He looked at me and said, "Woman, has no one condemned you? Where are they now?"

I buried my head and said, "They're gone, sir."

And then came the words that I never, ever expected to hear. "Neither do I condemn you."

Right then, I just wanted to run away in my shame. I wanted to hide, but there was something in His eyes, something that would not let me leave His presence. That's when He said gently, but with a quiet strength, "Now, go and sin no more."

"Go and sin no more." That was the first time in my entire life that anyone had given me another chance. People had just always expected me to be the same old girl caught in the same sin, and I believed it. Now this man, Jesus, drew me to change. He expected me to be different. I have never been the same since I met Him.

To be totally honest, I don't think there is any way I could go back to my lifestyle of sin after what He did for me. That day, He not only saved me from death, but He gave me a new life. He gave me a second chance at life.

MISERY MEETS MERCY

St. Augustine said that there is probably no greater picture in the Bible of how misery meets mercy than the story of the woman caught in adultery. Misery was everywhere, but mercy prevailed.

At times we find ourselves in miserable situations brought on by bad decisions we've made. Can you imagine the pain in this woman's heart? Can you imagine what ran through her mind as she was caught in adultery? It is shameful enough to be caught in a little white lie, but being caught in the very act of adultery had to bring her overwhelming shame.

The Pharisees thought this was a great way to trap Jesus. They tried their best to get Jesus in a tight spot. They wanted to put Him in a situation where He might slip up.

Jesus continually gave truth to common people, and the religious leaders did not like that because they wanted to be in control of truth. They wanted the picture of God to be painted their way. But Jesus arrived on the scene and started making the truth clear. They knew that if people continued to listen to Jesus, they would no longer tolerate being controlled by the Pharisees.

So, they came up with a plan to try to trap Jesus. What they didn't understand was that Jesus always knows what's going on.

Jesus was teaching when the Pharisees came in with this woman they had caught with someone else's husband. She had no defense. She was guilty, and according to the law, she was worthy of death. The religious men were eager to stone her.

It gave them great pleasure to put Jesus in the middle of their controversy. If He allowed the adulterous woman to be executed, He would no longer be the friend of sinners, and people would stop listening to Him. If He let her go, they could accuse Him of transgressing Moses' law and they could silence Him by putting Him to death. Either way, Jesus would be silenced.

The compassion of Christ is like a deep well. He didn't react rashly, but rather remained silent and slowly stooped down and wrote in the sand with His finger. He knew exactly what to do when He was faced with an impossible situation. Some say He wrote a list of the sins of the men with stones in their hands. Perhaps He was writing the names of the men who had sinned with this very woman. After all, how had they managed to catch her in the act? And where was the man she had been caught with?

ALTHOUGH GOD REJECTS OUR SIN, HE NEVER REJECTS US.

We don't know what happened, but nowhere is the Lord's rejection of sin and His acceptance of a broken sinner more beautifully displayed than in this story.

Although God rejects our sin, He never rejects us. This woman was thrown down in a heap in front of Him. As Jesus looked around, a hoard of finger-pointing religious leaders were scowling at her with clenched teeth. "Look what she has done. Moses says she must be stoned. What are you going to do, Jesus?" They were not truly concerned with the sin, nor were they concerned about the woman. They were consumed with their attempt to trap Jesus.

You can bet that this woman was thinking, *If I could only turn the clock back. Why did I get myself into this? I knew better. Why did I do it? Why, why, why?*

Now she was condemned to die. She looked up from the ground, and saw her accusers surrounding her, ready to carry out the execution. She had no defense. She was guilty and deserved to die, and she knew it. She also saw Jesus stooped down writing in the sand in front of her.

When Jesus finally spoke, He gave a diamond of hope to anyone who had ever been caught or found guilty of anything. "He that is without sin among you cast the first stone."

In essence, He said, "Okay, go ahead and execute her. Everybody line up, and the one who is without this type of sin, get in the front, and we will work back from there." He leaned down and began to draw in the sand again, and their consciences convicted them.

Then there was a great disappearing act. The woman looked up to realize that the men had gone and no stones had been thrown. She knew she was guilty, and she knew what she deserved. Now the jury was gone and she was ushered into the Judge's chamber with the only One who could judge her. Her Judge was sinless, which meant He was the only One qualified to carry out her execution.

Jesus said to her, "Has no one condemned you? Where are your accusers?" She looked at the sinless One and said, "They're gone, Lord." She didn't defend herself. Instead, she just threw her case on the mercy of heaven.

Jesus looked at her and said, "Neither do I condemn you. Go and sin no more. I am setting you free to leave this life of sin. I am giving you a pardon from heaven. Don't go back to that life of sin."

Then Jesus turned to the stunned bystanders and said, "I am the light of the world. He that follows me shall not walk in darkness, but will have the light of life" (John 8:12). Jesus was saying, "No more do you have to walk in the despair of darkness. You can walk in the light."

There are really no secrets in life. Everything surfaces eventually, and there is always a price to pay when you are involved in immorality. It is inevitable. You cannot be addicted to sin without it affecting your life. Sooner or later it will have an impact, not only on your life, but also on the lives of others around you. There is nothing you do that will remain a secret.

This story also shows us that we really cannot successfully conceal our own sin by exposing the sins of others. That is the worst kind of religion. The Pharisees in this story were quick to accuse the woman of sin, yet they were hiding sin in their own hearts.

The loudest accusers are usually just hiding their own vile secrets. The person who likes to push the sinner out in front is usually thinking like the Pharisees, *"Maybe if everyone is focused on this adulterous woman, they won't notice the things in my heart."* We may be able to fool people around us by being so brash about our own personal holiness, but we cannot fool the eye of heaven.

Another lesson in this story is that Jesus in no way condoned this woman's sin. Jesus knew the ruin of moral decay. He knew what she had been through. He knew the loneliness of her heart. He knew that sin had not satisfied the longing in her life, and that it had done nothing but create more problems and more heartaches. Many of us could tell our own story of the pain associated with the bite of sin and the hurt that it creates.

A NEW LIFE OF FREEDOM

Jesus offered her a new life, and He is the only One who could do it. He offered her freedom. He stood between the law that demanded her execution and the grace of forgiveness.

Jesus is the only One who stands between the two camps of law and grace. He is the bridge of salvation to mankind. Jesus stood as the bridge, holding out His hands to a woman who, while being found guilty of breaking the law, was a candidate for grace. He offered her forgiveness and deliverance. All she needed was to turn from her sin and begin to walk in freedom.

Jesus stood up for this guilty woman when others wanted to stone her, and He will do the same for you. The real truth is that He did it for all of us by dying on the cross. Now there can be forgiveness and cleansing because of His sacrifice.

YOU CAN BE FORGIVEN AND LIVE FREE.

This story is a song full of rejection and abuse. It tells of overwhelming guilt and shame. Shame is hungry. It consumes many people's lives every day. But this is not just a song of shame and rejection; it is also a song of grace gone wild. Jesus told her what He tells each of us today, "Go and live free. Don't go back to the dark. Live and thrive in the freedom of that light."

I sometimes wonder how often she thought about this encounter later in life. Maybe as she prepared dinner, a husband walked in, and behind him walked two little boys. I wonder how often she whispered, "Thank You Jesus, for giving me another chance."

I wonder how many self-righteous onlookers pointed and whispered, "That's the one. Do you remember when she was caught in adultery?" She still has the label of "the woman caught in adultery" over two thousand years later. Perhaps someone has put a label on you. The important thing to know is that you can have a turning point away from sin and all the guilt and shame that comes with it. You can be forgiven and live free. Regardless of your guilt, you can find your turning point in Jesus' words, "Neither do I condemn you. Go and sin no more."

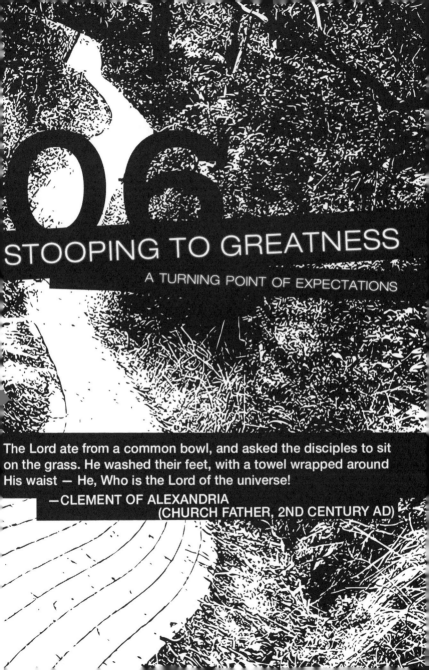

06

STOOPING TO GREATNESS

A TURNING POINT OF EXPECTATIONS

The Lord ate from a common bowl, and asked the disciples to sit on the grass. He washed their feet, with a towel wrapped around His waist — He, Who is the Lord of the universe!

—CLEMENT OF ALEXANDRIA
(CHURCH FATHER, 2ND CENTURY AD)

There's a story in John 13 that shows the disciples encountering a difficult turning point. Jesus is nearing the end of His public ministry. In that final week of training, He is trying to make sure His disciples really have a grasp of the most important things He has taught them.

Jesus knows that the sand in the hourglass is falling and that in just a few hours He will be crucified for the sins of mankind. He gathers His disciples together in a little place now known as the Upper Room.

There, Jesus will introduce the Lord's Supper and give the disciples a new way of looking at the cup and the bread. Tonight, they'll take communion together, and then He will talk to them about the things that are most important to Him.

As they gather together, there is a dispute among the disciples that fills the air. After three years of being together and listening to Jesus teach, they're fighting about which of them is going to be the greatest, and who will be preeminent among them. Their expectations are still so far off from where they should be.

A LESSON IN SERVANTHOOD

According to custom, when people entered a home, they were expected to wash their feet. The dust and grime of the filthy roads they walked made this necessary. Usually the lowest servant was assigned the role of foot-washer, but no servant is with them on this night.

The disciples are so concerned about who's going to be the greatest that none of them even wash their own feet when they arrive in the Upper Room. They all know that it needs to be done, but each of them walks right past the basin and towel that sits by the entry.

Everybody walks in and in effect, says, "I'm not doing that. It's not my job. Someone else will take care of it. I'm sure no one expects *me* to wash *their* feet. Where's the servant?"

Jesus walks in and sees the towel and basin still sitting there. He looks around the room and sees all His disciples with dirty feet waiting to eat the Passover. He also hears them bickering about who is going to be number one. So, He takes the towel and basin, kneels down, and begins to wash the crud of the world from the disciples' feet.

There's no doubt that Peter feels terrible about the whole deal and is thinking like the rest of them, *I wish we had done that. He is our Rabbi; we're His students; and He is washing our feet.* Then Peter's thoughts spill out from his mouth. "Lord, You can't wash my feet. What are You doing?"

Jesus looks up at Peter and says, "If I do not wash your feet, you have no part with Me." In other words, "If I cannot cleanse you by My forgiveness, you will never be able to come into My kingdom. You've got to let Me cleanse you. You can't earn it or work for it."

Jesus continues around the room and washes all their feet. When He finishes, He gets up and dries His hands and puts His robe back on. Our Savior, moments away from being betrayed, puts away the basin of dirty water, looks at His chosen twelve, and says, "Do you understand what I just did? You call me Teacher and Lord, and you are right because it's true. And since I, the Lord, your Teacher, have washed your feet, you ought also to wash each other's feet. I have given you an example to follow. Do as I have done to you."

He continues on, "The truth is that a servant is not greater than his master, nor are messengers more important than the one who sends them."

In essence, He looks at them and says, "After three years, we should not still be dealing with this. If we're going to get this gospel to the world, then you must settle this issue of being a servant. You guys have got to quit all of this fighting about which of you is the greatest. We're never going to be able to get anywhere if you do not understand that it all comes down to the heart of serving. I have called you to be servants. I'm not giving you a title, but a towel."

Then He brings it all down to this; "You know these things; now do them. That is the path of blessings. I've brought you along for three years because I need you to become servants. Serving is how you'll sustain what has been started over these three years."

A NEW COMMANDMENT

He pauses, and with a tone that let the disciples know He was about to say or do something very significant, He says, "I give you a new commandment." The disciples are locked into Him now, because they know what He's about to say is going to be huge.

With all of their attention focused on Him, Jesus spells out the new commandment. "Love each other. Love each other just as I have loved you."

From our viewpoint today, we can understand this to mean the love He showed us on the cross. But to the disciples on this historic night, He hasn't yet shown His love to them by going to the cross. He is telling them to remember how He lived, loved, served, and cared for them, and to do the same for each other.

IT IS OUR LOVE FOR ONE ANOTHER THAT WILL CONVINCE PEOPLE THAT WE ARE HIS DISCIPLES.

He says, "Just as I have loved you, so you should love each other. Your love for each other will prove to the world that you are My disciples." It is not your grasp of theology, not any spiritual, mystic, abracadabra movements, and not the way you carry yourselves. It isn't your haircut, your clothing style, the address of a church, a star of the faith, or a denomination. It is our love for one another that will convince people that we are His disciples.

Jesus is trying to change their expectations. They are ready to *be served*, but they should be ready to *serve*. I think some of the reason for this is that the disciples thought they were going to establish the kingdom by the sword. They just knew that Jesus was going to let them overthrow their Roman oppressors.

After supper, they leave the Upper Room and head to the garden. Judas shows up with a bunch of soldiers and kisses Jesus on the cheek. Here's what tells me the disciples were looking for a fight: Peter is there with his sword, as if to say, "I've been waiting for this moment." The Bible says that Peter takes a swat at a guard and cuts his ear off. Have you ever thought about that? He cut off the soldier's ear. I've never seen anybody in a fight try to trim somebody's ear, so I think Peter was trying to take the guard's head off, and when he ducked Peter clipped his ear. Peter wasn't just going for an ear; he wanted to kill the man.

He still thought that the kingdom was going to be established by a sword. His expectations were still out of line. Just a few minutes before, Jesus had handed Peter and the others towels and said, "This is how My kingdom is going to work—a servant's towel."

WHEN YOU START SWINGING A SWORD, PEOPLE AROUND YOU EITHER RUN FROM YOU, GET WOUNDED, OR FIGHT BACK.

Some people try to run their marriages with a sword. When they're newly married, they treat each other with such kindness. But, after a while, rather than serving and encouraging each other, they allow their kindness to be replaced with a sword. One starts trying to force the other to do things their way, and the tongue starts to become a sword. When you start swinging a sword, people around you either run from you, get wounded, or fight back.

It doesn't work in a marriage, and it doesn't work in the kingdom of God. The kingdom of God is not about us telling everybody how to live. It's not about us saying, "We're right and you're wrong." Jesus' message to the disciples in the Upper Room was that His kingdom would be established through loving and serving.

Talk about a change in expectations! They're thinking they're going to take over the world, and they find out that they have to wash the world's feet.

I believe the disciples also thought that Jesus was going to give them thrones to sit on. After all, they had been with Him three years. They've slept countless nights out under the stars, and they've eaten crickets and wheat. Jesus just *had* to put them in the palace. It was time to bump it up a little bit.

As a matter of fact, the mother of two of the disciples gets involved and asks Jesus, "When You come into Your kingdom, can You give my boys a couple thrones right by You? My babies would look so good on thrones."

Jesus says to her, "Do you have any idea what you're asking Me? I do not give them a throne; I give them a cup. It will be a cup of betrayal—a cup of isolation. It will be a cup of pain, and they will indeed drink it." When you follow Jesus, sometimes you pay a price.

YOU CAN NEVER GET SO SPIRITUAL THAT YOU NO LONGER HAVE TO SERVE OTHERS.

All too often we're seeking a throne and not a basin of water and a towel. And if you succeed in finding a way to live your life sitting on a throne commanding everybody else to serve you, you will find that it leaves very little room for those people to love you on their own. And what's worse, you'll live your life being paranoid that somebody is after your position.

Sometimes this happens in churches too. Someone gets put in a position of leadership and they begin acting like they are in charge now, so everybody else needs to take care of them. Everybody should serve them. They think that if they get real spiritual, they'll no longer have to serve.

You can never get so spiritual that you no longer have to

serve others. It's really quite the opposite. The more in touch you are with God's Spirit, the more you'll have a passion to serve the people for whom Christ died.

It all comes down to the fact that Jesus wants His disciples to be people who know Him and make Him known. Our commission from Jesus is to know Him and make Him known. That's what we live for. It's that simple. We need to allow our expectations of our own advancement and our own agendas to die. And we need to begin devoting our lives to spreading the message of Jesus' love, and to know Him and to make Him known by serving others and not just ourselves. It's about His expectations, not ours.

His plans for you are far greater than you can possibly imagine. He has great expectations for your life.

07
COMPLETING THE TURN

I'll never be the same again,
Because You loved me.
I'll never be the same again,
Because You saved me.
Now my life will be all You want it to be.
I'll never be the same again.

—DELYNN RIZZO, FROM THE SONG "WONDER OF THE WORLD"

We've looked at several turning points in this book. They come in all shapes and sizes, and they hit you when you least expect them. They can be confusing, frustrating, thrilling, or frightening. The fact is, we don't control much about how or when turning points come.

We do, however, get to decide what comes out of a turning point. Do we become better or bitter? Are we closer to God after the turn, or further away? Do we refuse to cross through the turning point, or do we allow God to take us to the other side? Do we embrace the turning point, or do we pass up an opportunity to start a chain reaction that helps people for generations to come?

The whole thing comes down to surrender. It is about faith and obedience. If we will obey, we'll find the experience of going through a turning point to be rewarding when it is all said and done.

Faith isn't something that lets you tell God what He needs to do for you. Faith is our pursuit of God's way, God's time, and God's plan because it isn't about us, it is about Him. Obedience is the expression of the strength of our faith.

Sometimes a turning point is a test, and if we don't pass it, we have to take it again and again until we do pass it. What determines whether we pass or not is whether we act out of faith and obedience to Him.

It is so worthwhile to see turning points for what they are: opportunities for God to draw us closer to Him.

Sometimes a turning point is just for us, like it was for the woman caught in adultery. Sometimes a turning point is for us and our household, like it was for the royal official. Sometimes a turning point is for our entire community, like the man on the other side of the stormy lake. Ten cities heard the Gospel because of his turning point. Sometimes a turning point is for generations to come, like the turning point the disciples had in the Upper Room. Often, turning points are a combination of all of these.

When the woman caught in adultery walked away from Jesus, there's no doubt that there were people who felt the repercussions of her life-change.

TURNING POINTS ARE OPPORTUNITIES FOR GOD TO DRAW US CLOSER TO HIM.

When Jesus taught the disciples that their expectations should be to serve and not be served, it made a splash with a ripple effect that is still being felt today.

The ultimate turning point is the cross Jesus died on. It affects every human that ever lived or ever will live. All of mankind was changed in that one turning point. Every turning point requires obedience. Jesus humbled himself "even unto death," the Bible tells us. He prayed the ultimate prayer of faith and obedience, "Nevertheless, not My will, but Yours be done" (Luke 22:39).

The cost in terms of suffering and pain can be very high

in life's turning points. But the rewards for handling them in faith and obedience can be far-reaching and overwhelmingly worth the cost.

Have you come to the point that you want to accept Jesus as your Savior? If you're there, you're facing a turning point. The Bible makes it clear that whoever calls on the name of the Lord will be rescued.

All you have to do is turn your life over to Him. Just tell Him that's what you want to do. Jesus has already died for you, and He is ready and waiting for you to come to Him.

Tell Him something like this:

> *"Jesus, I need You to take over my life. I confess that I'm a sinner and that I need Your forgiveness. I believe that You died on the cross for my sin and rose again for my salvation. I want You to turn my life around and be in charge of things from now on. Thank You, Jesus."*

Today could be the day you start your turning point. Give Him the controls of your life and see what incredible things He has in store for you.

Dino Rizzo has been senior pastor of Healing Place Church in Baton Rouge, Louisiana, since he and his wife DeLynn founded the church in 1993. God has blessed them with three children: McCall, Dylan, and Isabella.

As a young pastor with a passionate calling to bring healing to hurting people, he inspires Christians to step out of their safety zones, abandon their fears, and connect to others with bold love. He encourages everyone to find what it is that makes them come alive so they can become the people God created them to be. But when all is said and done, touching the poor and hurting is his consuming passion.

This is reflected in the heart of the people at Healing Place Church, where God has built an incredible team of people who love Him and love one another, and work tirelessly from six different campus locations to reach their community and world with the hope of Jesus. Whether it is giving water away at a busy intersection, cooking hundreds of thousands of meals for hurricane evacuees, tuning up cars for single mothers, or hosting free medical clinics, the people of HPC love to serve.

One of the church's campuses is located in Donaldsonville, Louisiana, which is one of the poorest areas in the entire country. The campus has been a place where dreams come alive. Serving the people of that community over the last three years has resulted in God's blessings and hundreds of opportunities to touch hurting people with His love.

As worship pastor, DeLynn Rizzo leads the church into an experience of worship that expresses authenticity and total devotion to God. The blend of excellence and passion to worship God in spirit and in truth creates an environment that allows for a deep connection of the Holy Spirit into people's hearts. Many lives around the world have been touched through several CD recording projects that were birthed from this heart of worship.

Dino and DeLynn have a love for people all over the world who are hurting. Peru, India, Zimbabwe, Swaziland, Mozambique, Italy and Brazil are all countries where they have an especially strong connection. Much of the work they are involved in is with the poorest of the poor, including thousands of AIDS orphans and vulnerable children.

The fire that burns in the hearts of Dino and DeLynn Rizzo and Healing Place Church is for hurting people; whether they are rich or poor, regardless of nationality or race. Their mission is clear—and they're living it out everyday—to be a healing place for a hurting world.

VISIT DINO RIZZO'S BLOG AT

WWW.DINORIZZO.COM

HEALINGPLACECHURCH
A HEALING PLACE FOR A HURTING WORLD

FAITH // COMMUNITY // FAMIL
ONE CHURCH. MANY LOCATIO

// call us at
225.753.2273

// send mail to
19202 Highland Rd
Baton Rouge, LA 70809

// visit us online at
HEALINGPLACECHURCH.ORG